weed

Spiders

By Theresa Greenaway
Photographs by Chris Fairclough

RSVP
RAINTREE Steck-Vaughn
PUBLISHERS
A Steck-Vaughn Company

Austin, Texas

Published by Raintree Steck-Vaughn Publishers, an imprint of Steck-Vaughn Company.

Acknowledgments
Project Editors: Gianna Williams, Kathy DeVico
Project Manager: Joyce Spicer
Illustrator: Tim Hayward
Design: Ian Winton

Planned and produced by Discovery Books Limited

Library of Congress Cataloging-in-Publication Data
Greenaway, Theresa, 1947–
Spiders/by Theresa Greenaway; photographs by Chris Fairclough.
p. cm. — (Minipets)
Includes bibliographical references (p. 30) and index.
Summary: Provides information on the identification, life cycle, and habitats of spiders, as well as on how to collect and care for them as pets.
ISBN 0-8172-5589-3 (hardcover)
ISBN 0-8172-4206-6 (softcover)
1. Spiders as pets — Juvenile literature. 2. Spiders — Juvenile literature.
[1. Spiders as pets. 2. Spiders. 3. Pets.] I. Fairclough, Chris, ill. II. Title.
III. Series: Greenaway, Theresa, 1947– Minipets.
SF459.S64G74   1999
98-34069
CIP   AC

2 3 4 5 6 7 8 9 0 LB 02 01
Printed and bound in the United States of America.

Words explained in the glossary appear in **bold** the first time they are used in the text.

Contents

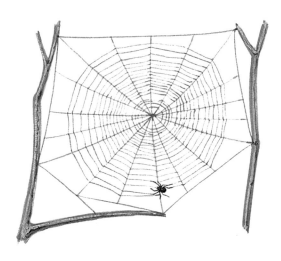

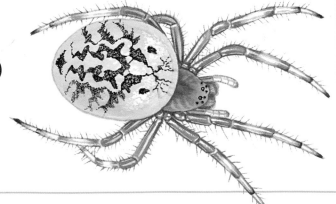

Keeping Spiders

Spiders make interesting minipets, and they are easy to keep. Some spiders may move right into your room and make a web in the corner by a closet. Others will have to be tracked down. But this is not difficult, because spiders live almost everywhere.

Do you know how to tell a spider from an insect? Just count its legs.

An insect has only six legs, but a spider runs around on eight. A spider's body is divided into two parts, joined by a narrow waist. At the front is the head and all eight legs. The back part is the spider's abdomen.

How spiders see

Spiders have poor eyesight. Most spiders have eight small eyes. They see only by detecting changes in darkness and lightness.

At the tip of the abdomen are tiny spinnerets. Most spiders spin webs with silk from their spinnerets. Spiders' webs are traps to catch their prey—insects and other invertebrates.

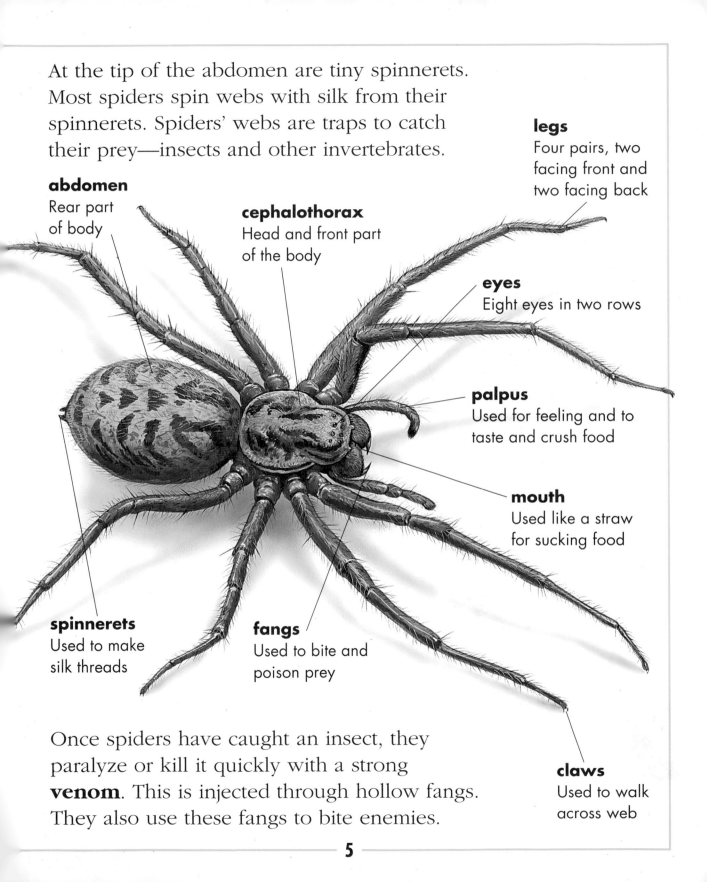

abdomen
Rear part of body

cephalothorax
Head and front part of the body

legs
Four pairs, two facing front and two facing back

eyes
Eight eyes in two rows

palpus
Used for feeling and to taste and crush food

mouth
Used like a straw for sucking food

spinnerets
Used to make silk threads

fangs
Used to bite and poison prey

claws
Used to walk across web

Once spiders have caught an insect, they paralyze or kill it quickly with a strong **venom**. This is injected through hollow fangs. They also use these fangs to bite enemies.

Finding Spiders

Spiders live wherever they can catch enough food to eat. Once you start looking for spiders, you will be amazed at how many there are. Begin by searching your house. A basement is a good place to look for spiders that prefer darkness. But you will also find spiders on windowsills and high up in the corners of living rooms.

▼ The water spider carries air down between its back legs and stores it in a dome of stretchy silk.

Outside, spiders live on lawns, in walls and flowerbeds, and under forgotten flowerpots. They live on tree trunks, in garden sheds, and in woodpiles. Spiders live in mountains and in caves. They live in tropical rain forests, cities, and semideserts. A few kinds of spiders have even learned how to live underwater in ponds.

During your spider hunt, you will often come across large webs, with the occupant nowhere in sight. Look very carefully. Is there a tunnel of web leading down to a hiding place? Is there anything nearby—for example, a rolled leaf—under which the spider could be hiding?

Try gently touching the web with a blade of grass. This will make the spider rush out to investigate and reveal its hiding place.

▼ Some spiders spin thick sheets of web in corners. If an insect touches the threads of this web, the spider runs out quickly from its hiding place and traps it.

▼ A hammock web is a maze of silk threads and trip lines. Any insect falling into it cannot escape quickly enough from the spider, who runs easily over the surface and bites its prey.

▼ Orb webs are the perfect trap for flying insects. The spider chooses a clear space between plants or buildings to construct the large web.

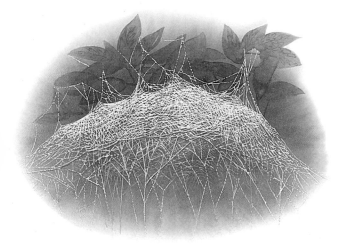

Spider Collecting

To collect spiders, you will need several small jars
or containers (with airholes in the lids), some labels,
a pencil, a small, soft paintbrush, and a notebook.
Try to avoid touching spiders with your fingers.

Spiders are fragile, with soft bodies that are easily
damaged. Use the paintbrush bristles to guide
the spiders gently into different containers.

Remember that spiders are hunters. So if you put more
than one in a container, they will eat each other.

Black widow

Even though it is quite small and shy, the female black widow spider has venom strong enough to kill a person. Fortunately, death is unlikely today because there is an **antivenin** available. Anyone bitten by this spider must go to a hospital emergency room to receive the antivenin.

Put lids on the containers, and make a note of where each spider was found. Number each container, and make a list of these numbers in your notebook. Alongside each write the date, where you found the spider, and what it was doing when you found it. If it had a web, try to describe it.

9

Identifying Spiders

Because there are so many different kinds of spiders, trying to identify each of your new pets may be tricky. A book of the common spiders found in your area will be a help.

Using the notes you have made, arrange your spiders into groups (there will be many different spiders in each). Here are four of the most common groups:

Orb weaver spiders usually live among plants. They spin round webs that look like wheels.

Running spiders run around on the ground. Some of them make silk-lined burrows.

Jumping spiders have the largest eyes and the best eyesight of all spiders. They are active hunters, jumping to catch prey.

Sheet-web spiders may live indoors or outdoors. They make a thick sheet of web with a tunnel leading to a hiding place.

▼ This photograph shows the three different stages of one jumping spider's movements.

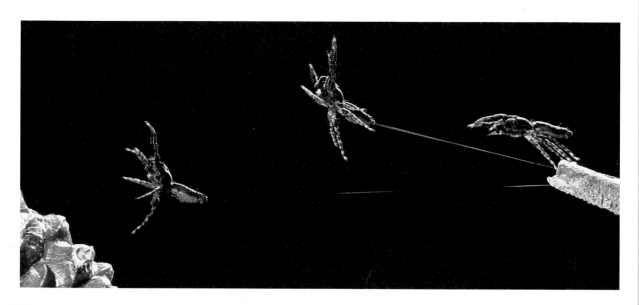

Long-legged cellar spider

One of the easiest spiders to recognize is the long-legged cellar spider. This harmless spider makes a web in the corner of a room. It has a thin body and amazingly long, thin legs. If you touch it gently while it is on its web, it will swing rapidly back and forth.

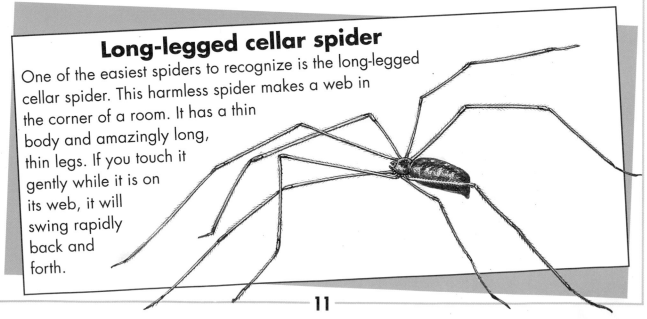

Homes for Spiders

You will need to use a different container to house each spider. An aquarium is best, so that you can see the spider clearly. Each aquarium should have a lid with airholes.

Don't forget that you will need to open the aquarium to put insects in for your spider to catch.

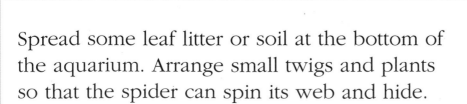

Spread some leaf litter or soil at the bottom of the aquarium. Arrange small twigs and plants so that the spider can spin its web and hide.

Purseweb spider

The purseweb spider makes a silk-lined burrow in the ground. This leads into a silk "purse" that lies along the ground. The spider waits patiently in its burrow. When an insect walks over the "purse," the spider bites it through the web and drags it down into the burrow to eat.

Running spiders and jumping spiders run over the ground or up walls to search for prey. So make sure that they have something they can grip onto with their feet. A piece of bark is ideal. Spiders that already live inside your house do not really need a new home. But you will have to persuade your parents not to dust away the spiderwebs for a while!

Caring for Spiders

Although spiders tend to look after themselves, they will need some help from you. Make sure that their containers are not placed in bright sunlight. Most spiders like some warmth, but they will die if they get too hot. If you are keeping the containers outside, make sure they are sheltered from rain. A spider will drown if its home fills with water.

You will need to provide food for your spiders. If you place flies in the container at regular intervals, the spider will do the rest. You can catch flies by placing some overripe fruit or jelly in a jar. Leave the jar outside. When there are flies inside the jar, put the lid on it.

At feeding time, gently empty the flies into your aquarium.

All spiders need moisture. So keep the leaf litter in their containers damp, but not soaked in water. If you have arranged small plants in the container, these will need some water.

Hiding and disguising

In the wild, spiders have lots of natural enemies. One way they protect themselves is by hiding, so that birds do not find them. They are often colored to match their background, which makes them difficult to spot. This crab spider from tropical New Guinea has a very strange disguise. It looks just like a fresh bird dropping. No **predator** wants to eat that!

Watching Spiders

One of the most interesting things about spiders is their ability to spin silk into webs. Watch your spiders closely to see how each kind makes its web.

Use a hand lens to see how a spider squeezes silk out of the tiny spinnerets at the tip of its abdomen. These spinnerets pull at the silk as it is produced, tugging it into long, fine threads.

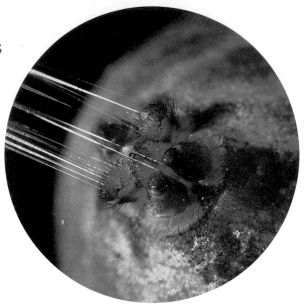

▲ A close-up of a spider's abdomen. The spinnerets are producing silk.

How spiders make their webs

1. A spider shoots a thread, which catches onto a twig. It then travels along the line, spinning as it goes.

2. Returning to the middle, the spider drops down to attach the line.

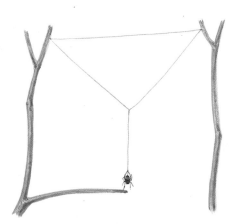

Once the web is made, the spider hides and waits for a victim. A single line of silk stretches from the web to the spider's hiding place. When an insect is caught in the web, it struggles and sends vibrations along the silk thread. The spider feels these vibrations and runs out to snatch its meal.

Look around outside, and see how many different webs you can find. See if you can spot thin trip lines leading from the web to the spider's den.

Clever catch

The net-throwing spider holds a small web between two pairs of legs and drops it onto its prey.

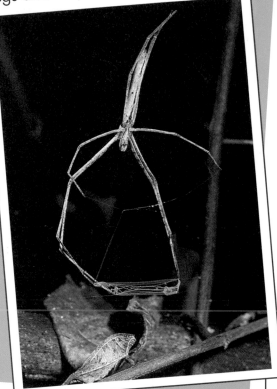

3. Threads are made around the edge and into the center.

4. The spider makes a spiral to strengthen the web and adds sticky threads for catching prey.

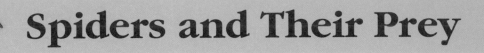

Spiders and Their Prey

All spiders are carnivores, which means that they attack and eat living prey, mostly insects. Different spiders eat different insects. Finding out which insects each kind of spider likes eating best is an interesting experiment. Try catching different kinds of flies or small invertebrates and putting them in the webs of your spiders. Take notes about what happens.

Spiders look busy when they are making a web. But much of their time is spent simply sitting quietly and waiting. Watch what happens when a fly gets stuck in a spider's web.

▶ This orb weaver spider waits motionless in its web until an insect becomes trapped.

The spider runs out of its hiding place. It sinks its fangs into the insect and injects venom that keeps it from moving. The spider wraps a thick band of silk around the insect. Then the spider starts to feed. Spiders cannot chew. Instead, they dribble **saliva** onto their food, which dissolves the prey. The spider sucks up the soupy insect juices.

▼ A spider makes sure its prey cannot wiggle free before the venom takes effect by wrapping its victim in a thick sheet of silk.

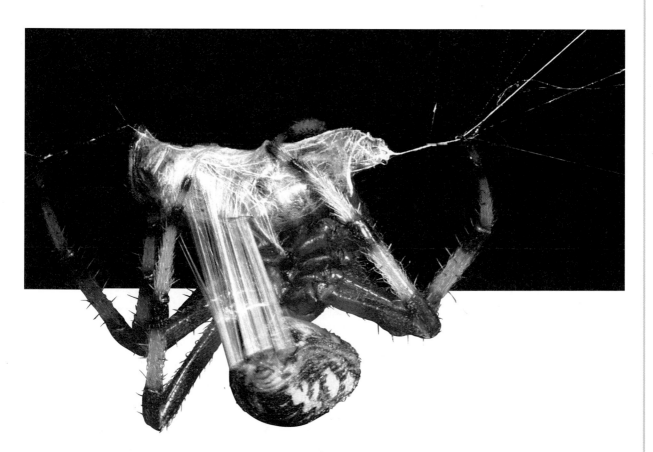

Spiders do not eat insects with an unpleasant taste, such as ladybugs. If a catch isn't good to eat, they either set it free or let it escape.

Multiplying Spiders

Spiders do not breed until they are fully grown. In order to get bigger, a spider has to shed its skin. The old skin, or **cuticle**, splits, and the spider struggles out of it. The new skin beneath is stretchy for a while, so it can expand. Shedding the old skin is called molting.

▼ This newly molted spider has just wiggled free of its old cuticle. It hangs from a silk thread until its new skin hardens.

▶ To avoid being mistaken for dinner, a male may bring a silk-wrapped fly for the female.

When a female spider is fully grown, she is ready to lay her eggs. She waits for a male spider to find her.

Spider courtship

Some males make signals with their legs, and others "pluck" the webs of female spiders.

Courting can be quite risky for a male spider. A hungry female spider may mistake him for a meal! Males are often much smaller than the females.

See if you can find a female carrying her egg sac, or guarding it in a tent of silk woven around grass stems. Collect these very carefully, and you may be able to watch the young spiderlings hatch. Keep the spider with her egg sac in a container outdoors. This way the spiderlings won't hatch and invade your house!

When Winter Comes

Winter is a difficult time for spiders. There are few insects for them to eat, and they have to find a hiding place free of frost. Many spiders, especially males, die not long after mating.

Female spiders may lay all their eggs in one batch toward the end of summer. They will guard them and then die. Other females may lay several small batches, then wait until after winter, and lay more eggs in the spring. Some spiders guard their eggs until they hatch. Others carry the little spiderlings around for a while.

▲ Wolf spiders cling to their mother until their second molt. If they fall off, they climb back using a thread of silk.

How long do spiders live?
The spider's average life span is 1 year. But tarantulas can live up to 30 years!

Spiderlings and surviving adults spend the winter in sheltered places, behind tiles or bark, under logs, or among the stems of huge tufts of grass. One way of seeing how many spiders there are is to go out early on an autumn morning after there has been a frost or heavy dew. Every spider's web will be covered with droplets of water or ice crystals. You will be amazed to see how many there are.

▼ A garden spider's web is transformed by a touch of frost.

Keeping a Record

To keep a record of your spiders, you will need a notebook, a hand lens, and a pencil. Try to find a book on spiders in your library.

Take plenty of notes about your spiders. Include details, such as which insects they prefer to eat, and how they catch and wrap up their prey. Note how many times your spiders molt.

Watch how spiders make their webs. When a spider spins a new web, it often eats the old one. This way nothing goes to waste.

▶ As this spider winds up its old web, it eats the silk. Silk is made of valuable protein, and the spider needs lots of protein to spin the new web.

Start a scrapbook, and paste in pictures and articles that you find in magazines. Once your friends and relatives know you are interested in spiders, they may start collecting for you, too.

Spiders have some quite amazing habits. You will be surprised just how interesting a spider scrapbook will become. You could even write your own spider quiz!

Hairy spiders

Under a hand lens, spiders look hairy. These thick hairs are not just to keep a spider warm. Each hair and bristle is extremely sensitive to touch, and to the tiny vibrations it picks up from the air and from the threads of its silk web.

Letting Them Go

The best time to catch and to keep spiders in captivity is in the spring and early summer. The weather is warm, and it is easy to catch insects for the spiders to eat. If they are well fed, the spiders will be fully grown by midsummer. This is a good time to let them go. They can find mates and lay their eggs before the fall sets in.

Choose a warm, dry day on which to release your spiders. Return the spiders to wherever you found them. Make sure you let them out somewhere sheltered. Otherwise, sharp-eyed birds will peck them up.

The tiny spiderlings have a great way of spreading out to find new places to live. Each little spider climbs to the tip of a stem or twig and releases a stream of silk into the air. This silk is pulled by air currents. When the silk is long enough, the spiderling simply lets go of the stem and floats away. The silk keeps it in the air. This is known as "ballooning."

Stranded spiders

Large house spiders trapped in sinks and bathtubs are a common sight on fall mornings. They are usually male spiders that have been searching for a mate. Once they climb into a sink, the smooth, slippery sides keep them from escaping. So they are stuck there until you rescue them. To help them out, push them gently into a container with a soft paintbrush.

During their fairly short lifetime, spiders eat numerous insects. Some of these insects, such as houseflies, are thought of as pests by humans. Now that you have looked after spiders, you know just how fascinating and useful they are.

Spider Facts

Green lynx spiders live in the southern United States and Central America. They live on plants, jumping from one to another. Their color is a useful **camouflage**.

This jumping spider is a back-to-front wasp **mimic**. If a bird attacks it, the "wasp" escapes in an unexpected direction.

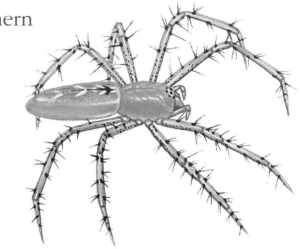

▲ A green lynx spider

Some rain forest spiders also mimic insects that have fierce bites or stings, such as ants or wasps.

There is an Australian spider that uses camouflage to look like a lumpy twig.

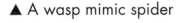

▲ A wasp mimic spider

Some people are absolutely terrified of spiders—even tiny ones! This uncontrollable fear is called arachnophobia.

Spider silk is amazing. It is made of **protein** and is stronger than a steel thread of the same thickness. It can stretch to almost double its length before it snaps. Even spiders that do not make webs always leave a silk trail behind them as a "lifeline." If they fall, they can climb back up the silk thread.

▲ This marbled orb weaver lays orange colored eggs in the fall.

There are over 30,000 different kinds, or species, of spiders alive in the world today. The tiniest spiders are no bigger than the head of a pin. The largest spiders are bird-eating, or tarantula, spiders from South America. Their bodies are 3 inches (8 cm) long, and their leg span is 10 inches (25 cm).

▼ A goldenrod spider

Goldenrod spiders can change color to match the flower they are hiding in.

Find out if there is a wildlife club or natural history club for children near you. Then, if you find it difficult to identify your spiders, you can take them along to show the experts.

Further Reading

Holmes, Kevin J. *Spiders*. Childrens Press, 1998.

Laughlin, Robin Kittrell, and Sue Hubbell. *Backyard Bugs*. Chronicle, 1996.

Parker, Steve. *Scary Spiders*. Raintree Steck-Vaughn, 1994.

Parsons, Alexandra, and Jerry Young. *Amazing Spiders* (Eyewitness Juniors). Random Library, 1990.

Ryden, Hope. *ABC of Crawlers and Flyers*. Clarion, 1996.

Savage, Stephen, and Phil Weare. *Spider* (Observing Nature series). Austin, TX: Thomson Learning, 1995.

Glossary

Abdomen The rear part of a spider or insect's body that contains its organs.

Antivenin A fluid that is injected into one's body to fight the poisonous venom received from a bite.

Camouflage The coloring of an animal that helps it to blend in with its surroundings.

Cuticle The outer layer of an animal's skin.

Invertebrate An animal, such as a spider, insect, crab, or slug, that does not have a backbone.

Mimic Something that copies the appearance or behavior of another kind of living organism.

Predator An animal that hunts another animal for food.

Protein One of a group of chemicals that are made by all living things.

Saliva The liquid produced in the mouth of an animal.

Spinnerets Organs in a spider or caterpillar that produce threads of silk.

Venom A poisonous substance that an animal injects into a victim.

Index

The publishers would like to thank the following for their permission to reproduce photographs:
cover (spider) © George McCarthy/Bruce Coleman, 4 B. Borrell/Frank Lane Picture Agency, 6 G. I. Bernard/Oxford Scientific Films, 9 Breck P. Kent/Oxford Scientific Films, 11 Kim Taylor/Bruce Coleman, 15 Ken Preston-Mafham/Premaphotos Wildlife, 16 Dr. Frieder Sauer/Bruce Coleman, 17 Ken Preston-Mafham/Premaphotos Wildlife, 18 Ken Preston-Mafham/Premaphotos Wildlife, 19 B.G. Murray/Oxford Scientific Films, 20 Rudie Kuiter/Oxford Scientific Films, 21 top Ken Preston-Mafham/Premaphotos Wildlife, 21 bottom Jane Burton/Bruce Coleman, 22 Ken Preston-Mafham/Premaphotos Wildlife, 23 Ken Preston-Mafham/Premaphotos Wildlife, 24 Kim Taylor/Bruce Coleman, 25 Ingo Arndt/Bruce Coleman, 27 Andrew J. Purcell/Bruce Coleman